WATER STAIR

Also by John Pass

Water Stair

John Pass

OOLICHAN BOOKS
LANTZVILLE, BRITISH COLUMBIA, CANADA
2000

Canadian Cataloguing in Publication Data

Pass, John, 1947-
    Water stair

Poems.
ISBN 0-88982-179-8

    I. Title.
PS8581.A77W37 1999   C811'.54   C99-911242-2
PR9199.3.P3435W37 1999

We gratefully acknowledge the support of the Canada Council for the
Arts for our publishing program.

THE CANADA COUNCIL | LE CONSEIL DES ARTS
FOR THE ARTS | DU CANADA
SINCE 1957 | DEPUIS 1957

Grateful acknowledgement is also made to the BC Ministry of Tourism, Small
Business and Culture for their financial support.

We acknowledge the financial support of the Government of Canada
through the Book Publishing Industry Development Program for our
publishing activities.

Cover photo by VCG/FPG-Canada Inc.

Canadä

Published by
Oolichan Books
P.O. Box 10, Lantzville
British Columbia, Canada
V0R 2H0

Printed in Canada

for Theresa
as ever

Contents

The Graces bathed here
and to reward the bath they gave
to the water the brightness of their limbs

The Greek Anthology

Back at the headwaters
the door was still there
to open, to close;
after a bath and shave
everyone recognized him
except the river
withering south
now only a reflection of a voyage
going home to tidewater . . .

Charles Lillard
Fraser's River

Invocation To The Character Of Water

Today, as past fate or motive it falls,

first light in the air
then accumulating weight, authority

I implore
                for thinking, and the writing hand

snow's impartial emphasis, expansive restraint.
What to do short of shovelling?

Though friends brave the driveway for my party
and arrive!
                And the laden firs, masters
of what, in one place, is attainable, strain
in their resins and sinews, their elastic greenery

to reply: a limb sporadically unsprung, waving . . .

        ❧

Just so come spring my clumsy paddle stirs, missing the J
stroke. Somehow afloat, dissolute as a Long Sloe Screw
in the sauna (ice-dregs over the coals)
I seek admission at the membrane, agency
in every cell. Let the roofs shed

what they must in my hearing and the molds
be under my nose. Let me through
with the native women in the first canoe
into the Stikine's hole into the glacier.

≈

And let me carry what comes to me
with equanimity, easily
with as smooth a countenance

the coffins
sucked by the North Sea from cliff-face graves near Cromer
sucked from *The Garden Of Heavenly Sleep*

as the biffys
flushed on the Assiniboine in flood into Winnipeg
flushed from up-river farms in the fifties.

≈

Hold my head under the overheard
and gossip's sprinklers.

Permit me the ancient, relentless return
of what has been taken deep and hidden.

I won't deny it. Nor the brackish bouquet
habitually acquired, particular
to where one wallows. A sip

or two of essentials is sufficient.
Certainly cataracts, be they directly

grief or pleasure. And the jocular creek
to knock the fisherman off his feet.
That swimming moonlight the night she showed me
our bodies' phosphoresence where we woke the water.
For my signature, your many inks.

I want to work and shape my way, but partially
I ascend and adhere to particles. Forgive me.
The disembodied babbling.

The bank collapsing and the silted flume.
The emissions stain on the marble lip.
The clear-cut bruise on the Naiad's hip.
The harbour's sheen that is not just pretty.

And the bathtub ring.
And the angle askew to the eye to things

plunged into you. That seem not to stand
on certainty. That waver.

Earth Day

Aswim as our senses dunk us
in rivers of phenomena
in the splash and surge

absurd to keep your feet
or to put your foot down

for murrelet, watershed . . .
but grasping for particulars

could thread that sailmaker's needle
of new moon, open and extend the loop

of lichen and cedar fibre
my son has hung from his ear

stitch with human gesture
snippets, earth-bits, to the earth.

Manet's *Le déjeuner sur l'herbe*
(a century, a continent away)
invented for this creek-mouth

its deep-throat Gothic upstream shade
beneath the leafy, leaning alders —
the ruined continuities

behind the dazzled picnickers.
Who'll say what a day's dream saves?
Tugged in eddies where you set

the kids' newt free
or ask permission of the mountain-ash
to trim its lower branches

or hear the CBC reporting frost on Mars —
volunteers step forward with their pamphlets.

Ducking from makeshift
shelter of billowing blue
tarp, between showers, beaming

they step forward
to sign us up.

Source

Backwards step by tai chi definitive
step in the deep moss into the backdrop
of old growth I go

a pantomimic parody of push.
Source for the moose is source for the panda.
Early Tibet? Early the drive

we took to Seattle seeking
zoo-solace, ore in the monumental
Art Museum. Ah, the one inconsequential

Matisse. The second-rate renaissance pieces
restored to fierce illumination anticipate
Mexican work in day-glo and black velvet.

Behold the alarm-protected Japanese tea-room,
the leaf-frogs dutifully shouldering leaves,
a worn Y of branch for the Emerald Tree

Boa. Ahead my wife and daughter stroll.
"Uh-oh," you're groaning, "some fashionable play
on works of art and nature comes." But no

I thought, "They are Canadian girls.
I *like* Canadians!" And Americans too — it's touching
how well we feel we do secure within

excellent facilities. At home
taking out the compost I spotted, yes
the moon! Most precisely Larkin's

"lozenge of love." His moon that was the whole
note of poetry in England, circa '74, so sadly
sugary on the tongue, a silver mist

a frosting, ephemeron . . . You see why
it suffered in translation (love sucks)
and my surprise to see it again

with that little shudder in the neck
and shoulders one gets sometimes taking a leak
tears springing to my eyes —

that reverberation of footsteps sounding
my grave. The intuition of hidden import
aroma is to baking. The tasty tang of those secretions

aperitif to love-making. Umbilical as the twitching wand
its shiver, older than the papyrus unrolling
the Nile. And I stepped back and sideways

to feel it fuller through the cedars'
lunatic fringe, dowsing blind as a back-rub.
This my empty plastic bucket, this

my wet and earthy hand from breaking
repeatedly, falls to the forgiving
forest floor. It was easy

leaving the city, likewise slipping
the retail leash at Bellis Fair Mall
harder backing away from the place

we gardened by starlight. But leaving aside
street people (and haven't we all)
we live right next door to our souls.

Near enough to neglect incompletely
those last endangered species
of ambition.

Waking The Well

" . . . and of youths,
Each with his maid, before the sun was up,
By annual custom, issuing forth in troops,
To drink the waters of some sainted well,
And hang it round with garlands. Love survives,
But for such purpose, flowers no longer grow . . . "

                    - Wordsworth

To the formal dark
(nocturnal, seasonal)

and to the darkly personal (dread's
dredges labouring 'round the clock)

day comes, processional.
The bloated little corpse floats up

or the whole moon, upon that penultimate
eve in April, tipped in

like medieval illumination
so exquisite and superfluous,

they dream it through, a first
feather of wisteria overhead, their limbs
around each other and the ancient stone
circumference, slumbering against the enormous
roots of the drinking trees.

They sleep through on the ground

since lost to us. No mysterious mossy cistern.
No Jack and Jill bucket wound childishly
expectant in the air. Light-years to count
the pebble down through its richochets
and final sounding echo

reflect upon contentment
and its deeper loss, make ceremony
of the winking surface.

Above the click and thrum of the submersible
pump, the sampling conundrum of the arsenic levels,
despite the inquest and the public hearing

it's almost sunrise on the lake.
An aluminum boat bumps idly
against the farthest, smallest island
where he tries too predictably to push past
her panties. The usual mindless whispering

in her ear and into earth's ear.
This entire intricate valley
of lake and hills not listening, resplendent . . .

the sun coming anyway onto the water, a majestic mercy,
model of coincidental fervor and reserve:
"Wake up. Wake up. I love you."

Sea Blush

No poem in May
so late in our love affair
with the earth, that battered marriage

can be entirely shameless, fearless
to do her justice, presuming to extol again
redundant beauty. Quickening even so

in the sudden names, seasonally
forgotten, spoken afresh, it whispers *speedwell*
to the miniscule blue-white sparks on the path

or leans in with a sliding touch
to the long cool muscle of arbutus
(a steadying hold, crouching lower)

to see up close the mauve-pink flower
awash in masses over the moss bluff
meadows near the water.

Tongue in her name each sundering first time
at sundown her look catches sea's deep colour

in a held breath recklessly lingers.

Kleanza Creek

How will we get up Kleanza Creek
who deserve it least, road-dozy, teeth afloat
on litres of coffee? We gotta stop somewhere

and this is it, exquisite twist
of water from the miniature gorge, a sheen
of pool behind the boulder, a riffle across

this pristine gravel
back-filled and levelled for picnic tables, grass —
the facilities operator even now sweeping
the parking area.

Its beauty is a pang, a duty
we get free. "Fish me," it burbles.
"Take the trail." But ours is a serious

recreation, the camping with kids denouement:
motel-hopping home. Re-load the camera
and back of that, let poetry do it.

Poetry goes where no-one follows anyway . . .

me and that utterly mythical beast, the reader
dreaming a way up Kleanza Creek
for our arcane two-step . . .

last-ditch landscape sleazes wheedling
"Show us, you'll be famous, really."
Open the cliff's cleft, the spigot

in the bedrock. Let's taste the salt-
lick in the alpine meadow

from the highway, the *open road*
before that delusion swung
off at every exit shopping

the next (some chalk-blue pot-hole
of the disappearing pick-up, the cast-off
gear, some well-bucket for the soul)

scoops me weeks later on a lake on "lack of . . . "
a cutthroat sudden on my line, a catch, a whine

in my voice at, "what grinds me
down is the lack of . . . "

get the trout in the boat and come
back to it: gracious, humbling

in-your-face reflection . . . "attention."

Aristotle's Lantern

When perspective is new who knows where we tend.
Piero's St. Mary Magdelen is realization
of purposeful form, a specimen.

The good work done, the halo in place
the act of grace subsumed in the state
"the curves in the regular bodies"

her hair remains bedraggled with oil
its emptied decanter transparently glass
her luminous weight, human

as any woman's who hurries, warm from her bath
in candlelight across the room, to bed, a lover.
"Beauteous night, O night of love, smile at our excesses,"

sings the whore in the dwarf's arms, departing . . .
Hoffman's captive soul in tow
a rival's blood on his hands
the gondola's lone lamp fumbling
with the architecture, the stupified water.

Cry him a river. I pinned my hope early
on Ping the duck, who, late and afraid
of the swishing stick, just punishment,
hid in the reeds as his family waddled
onto the junk on the yellow Yangze, at sunset.

Alone, disconsolate, he saw them go
but found them again by luck, downstream!
Though a man might have his balls chewed off
by another, at a guard's whim, in Bosnia.

At length, at last, past the fish-count shack
where the forest opens west to release us
past unnatural history, past the little wheeze
at the bottom of your breathing: salt-water.
And perhaps a crevice concealing
the urchin aria

named for the great teacher: orchestration
of forty skeletal pieces meshed
in muscle or ligament

for the synchronous movement
of five teeth, ever-growing, ever-ground
down on the rock, reaping algae. Appetite

insistent, blind to even the aqueous light,
couldn't be that virtuous striving, aspirant
form within the form: active soulful happiness.

Fresco, melody, story, faith.
A theory of evolution.

O the taste, the pleasure
as we lick and kiss each other there
grooming the metaphysics.

Twenty-three hundred years and counting.
The same observable mouth-parts, apparatus,

Cartier's Glossary

"At the end of the account of his first voyage to
Canadian waters there is a brief glossary of Indian
words, a *vade mecum* of empire: In that little
dictionary the first word is 'God' (for which the
Hurons had no term), the last is 'Sword' (for which
they did), and at the heart of the list, at the absolute
center of Cartier's testament, is the fatal word,
'Gold'."

– John D. Seelye, *Prophetic Waters*

The winter my asthma goes clinical
and the wandering shrews expire in number
along the trails and driveway edges, intact,
apparently healthy (of some nameless terror, it must be
some owl-shadow winging over . . .)

Bouchard goes south with the S word
and I start to get visits from Jacques Cartier.
"Jacques," I say, "what's finished won't sustain us,"
thinking of the house I've built, my remaindered titles
him turned back at the Lachine rapids, pyrite in the hold.
"So, what's next, eh," I ask rhetorically,

thinking to distract him with the joke
of the disproportionate maps. Lake Superior
in Hudson's Bay. Florida in Appalachia.
Then Radisson, La Vérendrye and the rest

taking the trade west
till the Co. went retail near Fort Langley.

26

But he's darkly serious, a Gallic melancholic.
That stagey faraway cast to his eye.
The cross on the headland over his shoulder.

It's Saguenay.

"Sacrebleu," I tell him, "a minor river only!
No high civilization. No fabulous Huron treasure hoard.
You mistook their propensity to please, to agree
when trading, to keep things going, to keep you happy,

for a real place.
C'mon, I'll take you fishing."

On the lake we catch nothing.
The watery reflections illusive as ever.
The deep jade of the shady bays unworked, unworkable.
"It ain't the Grand Banks, Jacques," I say
coming to my last lure, a red devil.
(I'm thinking 1534, you understand)

and he pulls out his glossary, revised, updated.
'Cod' reads the first entry, and half-way through,
that tired jibe at the country: 'Cold'. Well, okay

so there's no more wit
in the spirit world than ours
but now 'Word' is his last word, his horizon
a post-modern/biblical riddle.

I get schitzy, panicky, at this
as if in the orchard with the dormant oil
too late in the season, pushy
bright scraps of March sky escaping.
Dropped stitches of wren-trill.

Screwed up in the twist in the bud
of the careless moments, thinking, always thinking

how to bring them to bear, when needed
when the weight comes down
on my breathing, on my thinking
about my breathing . . .

"You mistake their propensity to please
to keep things going, for fantasy, your need only,"
he's saying (in surprising English) "mais régardez-moi

coming to that clearing, settlement
on the Great River of Canada.

She's a real place: here, eventual.
The only enigma her wild, untranslatable name."

The Lost Rivers Of London

"Sweete Themmes runne softly, till I end my Song."

- Spenser

Imperial pavements
and the hard tack to trackless passage and power
over water. The antique lust for it. Its instruments

rusting in the shallows, their shadows (irony, nostalgia)
reaching still. Each advance sequestered
in its romance (horse latitude or elfin grot)

the tortuous recourse upstream
to Paradise, New World.
Somewhere spilling forth, perpetual.

Somewhere divided and apportioned
directions, moral purpose . . .
improbable real geographies emerging

Serpentine. That duckpond somewhen
an arm of the Westbourne, a finger
of the Thames. Lamented, oh

and Hugo's sewers and Love Canal
one backwater backwash in the flush

steam-whistled in
of profit's sweet felicity.
Fair sailing and fond memory

on down her labyrinthine one-note whine, scream
of the coin-op social turbine, deep fluencies spun

off toward excesses in the air, new element
all space and signal, hugely static

sexless and invisible.

Gold Mine

So promises the highway sign
at the trailhead to the beach
but at its end a rusting dredge

on a bench of creek in its last meander west

is what was meant, icon
of our explicit history: another thing
done for money. Over the crest

full-frontal to the sea a later totem
languishes, column of wind-broken fir
or cedar carved and greying, a face
or two roughed in, enhanced

by round stones balanced
in the eye-sockets. It's a summer's work
at most and the carver's apprenticeship, the twist
and flip of dolphin atop the pole a first
lucky alloy of skill and inspiration.

I'd forgotten on our way down
to the gold mine my generation's
quicksilver work on the surface —
our summer on these beaches, disciples
of the neo-native. Shell worship.
Pebble worship. Those to-hand perfections
deserved it once of us. And confronting
the acres of breakers we dreamed

not only of accompanying
our wind-burned sun-burned salty naked selves
and lovers into the forest, into the townhouse
history had waiting. We leaned a little

to the luminous exposure
as it screens me now, here with my children, in-laws
and instant camera, panned out in thunderous haze
and brilliance: patina, slender vein . . .

Nozzle

Directed force is pleasure in effect
or promises, promises . . .

such that men cast massive
iron and brass hydraulics in pieces
mule-carted arid distances into gold country.

Every inch of Williams' Creek streambed
already worked down by hand to bedrock
the townsite risen fourteen feet
over tilled gravel —

they rode the nozzles like battleship gunners
to smash to rubble the Barkerville hillsides
for more bright f leck in the sluices.

Directed force is a primary pleasure
though tethered to myths of effort, profit
and leisure for exercise, and slave

to subtler energies and engines, buffalo clouds adrift
in herds of slow migration from the coast,
overlooked valleys greening
under the rhythmic swivel and kick of sprinkler systems.
Reaches of mist and rainbow above the timothy.

> The human metabolic scale
> from panic to despond
> is earthy only in middle registers

in the hands-on company of things
in campaigns of physicality
or that companionable delusion

of a place among them, our feet
on the ground, or our backs
to the warm barn shingle

the clouds a spacious reverie, a consolation
of release, and not the shapeless terror
of wild dissociation, vertigo

letting go
its trap-door, floor shadow...

Here, take this pressure-washer spatula
of sheeting spray to the mud-cake on your trailer.
In build-up, hold-back, manipulation
of the tip, flow

goes with us, shapely
makes a point, an edgy
blade, cuts

to, caresses, the finish.

Lure

One Day Out

I'm troubled by the city's tenacity,
its tight line to my life —

Good dry grass making me sneeze
and my eyes water, good sky,
good wind, good river,

let me be less careful
on the loose rock
at the edge.

Give me the cottonwood's grace
there, leaning from land, open
hands of her roots abandoned
to the air, fingers idle,
entranced in the current.

I want to go

deep. In my haste
the light lure flashes
on the surface of the fast water.

Wild Rose

A point on the lake
open with birch and wild rose,
endless forest at our backs.

The tents are up.
The fire has fed us and makes room
for our eyes and our talk in the dusk.

Plop

of toads a few feet
from shore. Mosquitoes.

Something every moment.

No-one else knows
exactly where we are.

Nights

What am I afraid of?
What would come for us?

On the first night
only the toads
and squirrels.

On the second the lake
rose
    to within
            inches.

On the third
a crash in the forest . . .

Ears wide, heart fast
to the baited darkness

I bite

my fingernails.
Hundreds of mosquitoes stunned

in the pre-dawn chill
cling to the netting.

In The Middle, Crossing

To escape the shoreline
of shadow and bleak cliffs

heads tucked in
to bodies tucked in

to the stroke, a sheet
   of lightning flung
      over us.

The approaching shore
choked with driftwood
and flooded undergrowth.

Beautiful B.C.

The photographer moves our fire twice
to get us and the length
of the lake behind

the mist, the wet wood smoke.

He's on his way up to Azure
with all his equipment.

Last Morning On Clearwater

The sun emerges gold
from cloud in the deep blue

of the lake
only the canoe
disturbs.

But for the noose
of shoreline, twined forest,
knots of mountain,

we're cast loose at the pivot
of sky upon heaven

some drifting load-
star hauling us

still
in the shimmer.

38

Junction

On the way back, more than halfway
home, at that unlikely spot just off
the highway near Lytton, a creek
mouth north on the Thompson
a mile or two

before that river swollen
blue with late-Spring run-off
from the Clearwater and Nicola
and a hundred other
snow-fed tributaries

dissolves in the muddy Fraser —

under a railway trestle, dwarfed
by the mammoth tar-spattered rocks
dumped there to support
the structure

from water thus made
quiet and deeper

we took them:
our only trout,
their cold lives

lightning in one hand,
the unthinkable

stone in the other.

The Thompson

" . . . and know that rivers end
and never end, lose and never lose
their famous names."
                            — Richard Hugo

Though we go down in the moonless dark,
faces blackened, bodies blackened, pitch torches

dipped to the river's surface
to preserve, even at the slippery edge, edgeways,
ourselves as a part of the dark, anonymous and whole . . .

though we darken the doors of the past, of the tribal
that humbly, as eager as children, as smug
and sincere as social workers

and would spear it
whatever it is in those moments leaps,
tailwalks, and we forget ourselves, and are native . . .

near is as near as it came. This river named
for a man (however accomplished) never here.
The Indians named in turn for the river.
The struggling approximations
eddy and go under. Adrift in the era

of the barbless hook, internal scar,
unending run and reel recovery,
people in black with brand
or nipple ring exact, bluntly
upon themselves, the violence of identity

40

or will appear, in cutting edge garb
and gear (Doc Marten/L.L. Bean camouflage)
at Spences Bridge. They've driven north-
north-east all day, through the Northwest
to dine in southwestern ambiance

on sole-meunière, determined
to be hip-high in the current by four a.m.
and outdo one another on the fly.

Vistas across
the river's pewter, a sudden
pungency of sun-struck sage,

dioxins flirting
with the steelhead's obtuse
but muscular purpose,

prime nostalgia for the old hydraulics —
utopian transformation. Come Spring
near Walhachin, feeble volunteering blossom
reaches for its last bees, their lost acres

of cashed-in, dried out orchard
tarped for ginseng, black
and taut with the sheen of new money.

Root and arranger of land-forms, life-forms,
depth-seeker, light dragger, mistress and miser
of the particles (gravel, profits, mists)
the river eludes its believers, giving its all.

The Caledonia

"On the Pacific slope of these first two maps he
penned in a watercourse he called the Caledonia
River, which he showed rising just west of his Boat
Encampment and curling southwest to enter the
Pacific between the Fraser and the Columbia. No
such river exists, and Thompson corrected this
mistake in the next version of his work."

— Jack Nisbet, *Sources of The River*

No such river exists
but persists in mystery, holds out
the mythic risk we have to take

to see past scenery, resource or habitat
the living whole. Where is it?
Canada's greatest geographer, cartographer
splashing off the map he's made

for headquarters, knew the headwaters
better than any, a Theseus of the threads
of river in the mountain mazes.

A trickster too? Laying down the traces
for copyright in fancy? Nearing truth
(that calamity of exactitude and consensus)

the singular author makes unique mistakes.
It's those we need

as a city needs a river
to reflect in deeper trances
its monuments, derelictions, dawn vantages

where brokers, lovers, street-kids lean
over to stare at the same disappearing thing
and on lifting their eyes see the edifice
of commerce stream and swim.

Its reach dreams an open mouth to the sea
teeming with nymphs, salmon, sweet destiny —
a hunch about Seattle . . . whatever we say
undammed but by the furbearer, windfall fir.

And in the cave of candlelight or laptop screen
compass and aerial camera can't discern
the line working, erring, essence gleaned

from alpine bog become freshet. Spring
as in a first step at the margin

jumping clear, in.

Hiker Ascendant At Mountain Creek

Thought creek
before he came to it. High
likelihood of subliminal

burble nothwithstanding (dictate
of the heat and the terrain)
as if obedient

to his summons its glint, glaze
of glacial water over

a log, pooling. Hands deep
his reflexive reach, scooped

splash into face and hair, shake
of the head. Nothing

interests the cerulean distance
given him coming up, headed

(upon rising, stretching as he is)
above headings, briefly focal

in a pantheon of peaks
point beside the point.

Fish Ladder

Yes, yes, the practicalities, take steps
or lose the biggest runs on earth come through
Hell's Gate, the spawn-rich possibilities
of waterfall-blocked Stikine tributaries.
But how we love the overlook

from where we blast our rights of way
above the torrent, and the view through glass
of resting pools for their ascent

we made. And this too, most
especially this: ubiquitous
freeze-frame of leaping fish
(those Tlingit dead seeking ice country

f-stopped at Super Natural
BC) icon of brochure

and wish as shrouded as St. Joan's
first putting on bright steel at Blois
or Scott's setting foot in Antarctica.

Antipodes. Limbless, errant muscle in the air
shook pennant of its element
held proud above a consequence

delayed, ever
suspended
            is what we dream
is what we touch each other with
like touching wood.

Adam's River

"Walter Moberly reports that, when he visited the
lake in 1865, he 'made acquaintance of Adam and
Eve, an Indian and his wife.'"

— Akrigg, British Columbia Place Names

Downstream ever further from our native
nowheres (paradise, wilderness)
we ooh and aah harder over
these sockeye come three hundred miles upstream

enamoured of their exactitude of instinct
sniffing out birth-scrabbled gravel and graves
as if home were the whole story

and not how far we've signalled in the circuitry
of the higher brain, how deep in its ocean
dropping off the ledges of the sonar.

Through all the known and unknown world
in widening reflection float
our theorems, overtures, internets

in the spacy self-consciouness
between available flavours, tasty speciation.

Anyone's buffed-up antique couple (singular, original
pre-parental statuary, isolate and looming
within each life's parentheses)

rubs uneasy shoulders on this crowded little bridge
with massive, loafing miracle, the amazing many
roughening, reddening the water, push

come to shove of populations
pursued, pursuing increase.

A hunger past naming, past feeding
firm-bodied flash and fluid mastery

bellies down best
against the streambed
against the steady current under
rib, under root, under rafter
gnaws inward . . .

leaves generation diddling
in its little hollow . . .

pleads synapse to the elements.

Dead Man's Float

I'd no need to lie face down
in the water, arms outstretched
to stay afloat in Lake of The Woods.

Being a chubby kid I could sit
among the log-like ten-year-olds earnestly drifting,
sinking, flailing

in the requisite six feet by the dock. I sat motionless
knees pulled up, beachball body tipped

back a little, head comfortably
pillowed on the surface. I could even pretend
(and did) to be smoking, right arm extended
to allow a quizzical, sophisticated gaze

at the mimed cigar. A couple of other campers
would spot me and shout to the counsellor, "look!"
And he would. At that age in that place

it was my singular, unique ability.
I outgrew it of course. Couldn't do it now

to save my life.

Mainstream

Pushing 50 in the fug and glut, burger
or brie in the gut, 181 channels under
the eyelids' stretch 'n' seal
and everyone you knew at 20
on welfare or TV or both, grunting blind

through intestines of bureaucracy, celebrity
or stranded with the weedy crap left standing
in clear-cut washed out gullies of a working life.
This is the shortest river in the world

where the mill squats farting sulphur
and profits sluice through degradation

to despair at warp speed. The fraught space
of a hangover enwraps the booty 'round — slime

under the draw-down and the ghostly silhouette
of the water's old progress in silt shroud

behind the dam. In the gaping mouths
of the great rivers dreaming is the ground-

up bough and bycatch, undone diversity
of gene and tongue, sing-song banter of working voices
clunking in the iron chink, screaming on the green chain.
Your mother's slack-jawed, bubbling mouth
post-surgery, won't survive it, mouth

which sang and read to you. You eating thing.
Settling pond and talk show can't redeem it. Nothing

the snow bleeding colour from sky and river
might clarify, can see you clear.

Vishnu Schist

for Charles Lillard, across the Great Divide

Under our pine in dry country
in August shade or February shelter
at ease on the pallet of its debris
(on seed, seed-husk and needle-bunch litter)

there is no further. The land deepens
as for those on the tour bus pulled over
at the canyon's rim. Blue scribble

of river beneath cliff-sheer
and the talus slopes' disquieting
angles of repose

is all the moving finger wrote
unintelligible, remote. The oldest rock

the deepest, uplifted layers exposed
are no more revelation than, adjacent
on the road in, that trailerpark
and graveyard. Smooth transition —

a trick with boxes,
simple disappearance, loss
of mauve skirting boards, lawn ornaments,

mock the *great nonconformity*, the shock
of paleozoic directly overlying
archeozoic rock. Someone must have painted

that abandoned homestead pink
after its collapse, its brilliance so emphatic
in the afternoon's strict sunlight

a smell of apples haunting
the sidehills' shadow.

And in the New Deal town below the dam,
hopeful stucco bungalows, tiny attached
garages with three-panel folding doors,
town hall at the summit of a tidy boulevard

make their short-focus gestures still
against the backdrop monolith. No further

no closer, comes the understanding, come
the glacial erratics to unsurprised
arrival, the *avataras* to conclusive

equilibrium

                    than under our pine in dry country
          as the land deepens, oceanic
millennia in time-lapse

crest and trough
of display, erasure.

Cave And Basin

The round-shouldered urinal
tall as the boy, CRANE
blue-veined on its porcelain
hauls him back

from his best cartwheels ever, smooth-
swung over-drop of one
foot,
    the other. From those successes
on park grass in sunlight
by the Bow river, back

he's beckoned to the echoing
public washroom where peeing
and shaking off the last few drops
he'd felt his cock out for something

further, and leans in again
to the urinal's cavern, its cool embrace

his body a bow to the further whatever
pulling . . . like everybody

lined up at the hot springs'
cave and basin historic site
foyer inside the mountain, sulphurous
rotten-egg odour and languid trickle
of stalactite to stalagmite almost touching . . .
everybody waiting

next to photos of the roofless pool in winter
snow to its blue steamy edges, guys playfully
snowballing girls in bikinis, stray shots
pancaked on the glass walls, about to slip . . .

predictable as the habitual slide
of men's eyes in once-over, one

woman to the next, each momentary mirage/
oasis, easy lay? Easy lie of some ease at least
for the mind's eye, mantric rub-down
for the clenched commute, transport, a way across town . . .

to the slick and slither of lovers
in the shower, his face all over her breasts
and belly going down, hands fumbling hot/
cold for the just-right mix, the venturing

ejaculate (its proteins stringy in the warm sluice)
catching on the stainless drain grate . . .

or ecstatic past entry
in sticky-eager little leaps from the hips' nudge

through the turnstile, for the ticket, the key, the click/
click one-on-one baby-making upreach
for a ready egg, a fit snug as the firm-fleshed

coming wonder in her birth
canal, as wild and precise
as kids outdoors in their own lives . . .

horsing around, flicking towels, ready to swim
but subdued a second emerging
from the mountain on the other side

past the upper pool, the hottest one
not for swimming (part natural rock
and part concrete ledges and hollows)
the spa pool contrived for the old and aching

dreamed-of mineral synthesis . . .
the kids subdued, nearly serious,
glimpsing those almost across

the great divide of gender, mortality,
species even,
                    their freakish fish bodies
mottled and flushed, accretions and expanses

of bone and flesh sporting floral
prints or enormous shorts
in their last shallows lulled and lolling.

Totem Creek

With fickle unlikely sunlight seeping
through Mt. Stephen's cowl of cloud

why wouldn't the living keep walking
the vague road behind the youth hostel

those Augusts the dog's water freezes
nightly in its bowl? And the old pits

and workings of placer mining in the bush?
Disappeared places, plank covers rotten,

awaiting footfall. Parallel lies
the creek beyond a stunted stand

of conifers sprung dense and skinny.
Glimpse its rush, its rumour

of bottomless potholes in chalky, swirling
welts on the surface.

Granite boulders barely rocking
in their limestone sockets

at depths the current no longer reaches
won't be lifted nor grinding deeper

their liquid columns in glacial till and hardpan.
Anchors, blank icons of inverted meaning

their cold (unlike the cramping cold
in the calves of kids kept standing
still in Moraine Lake or Maligne Lake
having their pictures taken forever)
is a breathless cold, a cold past feeling

its grimace smoothed, egged
toward effacement, recognition.

Water-colours

Using up the time
on the parking meter
I find myself looking
at prints in a bookstore.
What is it about them
makes me want to look again
at everything?

❧

A touch of new snow
on the forested mountain
slope, light as cloud.
I ache to be so
gentle with the world.

❧

There are the bare trees
dry with cold. Below them
the traffic struggles as the light
changes. I'm left at the wheel, waiting.

From the bedroom window overlooking
the orchard I can see more than ever
of the valley and the faraway
glimmering sea. On the ground
one apple keeps its colour
among the frosted leaves.

Always, in a way
it's a lie. As I recall
there were no water-colours.
There are the colours of the evening sky.

I waste the daylight
writing, lost in subtleties.
It's dark when I walk
near the stream not expecting
the sound of water.

Grassy Knoll

Eyes ever rain-shrouded or climbing the cloud-
break's revelation (coast mountains'
glacial, glorious backdrop highs)
what's to see in life-size rise

and fall, in fountains?
Their european lilt, refrain
of being's bright
essence and fresh flippancy
in sunny civic air

is puny, allegoric slush. For lift let's do
the after-math of sturdy stuff in steel
and glass, then slide imperiously fit

upon the slopes and seas. Beyond projections
of collapse pre-tax potential earnings surf
torrential speculation . . .

At Bridal Veil Falls near Hope's off-ramp
(rock-face forever dreaming under lace) no-one's
standing for the mist's kisses. At Takakkaw's stupendous

drop from cloudy ridge through fogs
of spray, you just can't see.
You just can't say.
Momentous and intangible these

commentaries mumble elsewhere, distant
thunder all the beach-dumb summer's day.
Dear knowing, travelled, smugly urban,
world citizens at last (at least

of TV history) can there be any grassy knoll
but that the shots ring out? The blood-soaked
cavalcade will slow and gasp and race
away below before you guess

it's not Dallas where I'm stretched
upon this pretty *mons* of lawn, plumbing the source.
A sort of seep and flow from somewhere, a sort of
incontinence of the earth

emerges down a wrinkle
of pebbled concrete faux-creek.
At base there's patio and pool, concrete columns
crowned with concrete squares and spheres, a pyramid.
An arch. A Parks' plaque naming

Andy Livingston. "I presume . . . " the pacing, wheeling
agent gushes, bullying the phone " . . . you've seen
the cuts, the rushes, the he on she? Who needs some
long safari into WE?" Nameless laid-off extras

straggle through this frame, city block
chopped from promo/porno culture.
It won't show pink (till sunset)

and drools too close the sink-hole heresy: incessance
of the hidden. Between the parking lots and plot
sustaining girls' field hockey, a statutory
holiday, a Sunday

in the soul's Geneva. GM Place
releases the fans. That Coliseum pastiche
is the library. To Chinatown for dim-sum?
Nearby the world-class strippers strum
low G. Will you fold a greenback under?

Flip in a loon? Tap the current no-show tune? Everything
is walk-on distance. From Skytrain overhead, hydraulic
whoosh and open pause of doors . . .

River Road

"Tao is a river . . . "

      – Lao Tzu

               . . . torrent and drift (passion's
pulse) but more the torqued cables bridging, barging.
Torments of adjacency, resistance. Strange shore

left stranger by history, camp followers. Camp-dogs
on the sniff for origin – a trickle here

of migration off the permafrost across plains, into valleys
of the first people moving. Dust there of their carts
and animals in Europe's summer riverbeds, Africa's. Asia's

oases twisting the silk road. Style and hesitation.
The stutter of beauty. Stone dolphins inter-
lacing up the water-stair at Villa Farnese.
Bernini's exultant interventions.

The Taj Mahal. The vanity of reflection.
Its heart-stopping artifice. Skid-marks
on our widening swerve

of blacktop above the guardrail.
In the sweep of concrete arroyo below, once

the San Gabriel River, drivers train
on the big rigs, the articulated buses.

Their shoulders ache from gearing
down, heavy steering, preparing for, fearing
the almost forgotten frisson on wet surface.

Upwelling welt/swirl on the Clearwater
that grabbed our canoe and spat it out sideways
against the sandbar . . . Detour. Digression . . .

Taste the best-remembered moisture
    in Arizona: watermelon juice
        on the yoke of her Mexican blouse, sticky
        on her throat, between her breasts . . .

        Still proud of her sun-burnished braids,
    her deep-set eyes, sunburst tattoo, high
    cheekbones, perfect teeth
a Xinjiang mummy removed from her dune

to the Institute's damp basement
mothers the long delay of body

a life is. So much of it high and dry.
This morning someone escaping

the commuter loop trudges
out past the signs on River Road
to the dyke's dead-end to sit
on a driftlog, head in hands, worries

loose with a boot-toe heat-
deformed pieces of bottle glass
from the mud-ash of a cold fire.
Poor dumb-ass last-ditch
self squatting there, clenched

and withheld in the open palm of the delta . . .

under the rain's relentless data
under the thrum and shudder

of pre-dawn flights lumbering
up in a blind fog over Lulu Island . . .

in your temples are softly drumming
(in our temples where hearing glistens

    busy with silt and sediment
    sounding the hulls and rounding
    the breakwater granite

unravelling the land-locked molecules)
in your temples are softly drumming

the babyish fingers and fists of the sea.

A Drink Of Water

Was it a dream
or waking
in the dark
makes you sob

so piteously?
Whichever, come on

we'll blunder through
the living-room
to the big window

squared-off at the moon. Shock
of light going into the familiar
bathroom greets us.

Here's a drink of water.

And another? Thirsty fish.
There swims an inkling

of a smile as your head goes down
on the pillow, buoyant

and deep.

Canal Flats / Grand Canal

Stand with Baillie-Grohman in 1882
on the shoulder of the Purcells gazing
east and north up the Rocky Mountain trench
but bear with his southwest intentions

for the arable flood plain near Creston
he'll sell once reclaimed from the Kootenay's high water
re-routing its headwaters here with a trench of his own

into the Columbia. Or step back a year into Venice
at Renoir's elbow as he fires up his colours' crucible
to melt the flowering gothic facades, the delicate loggias
into their original mercantile energies —

the bloods and golds of lucre and sunset and feeling
aflame where we live between sky and water.

Each knows flow, control, connection
from opposite poles of the Great Western Power Project
the heat and buzz at their backs building
on invention/reinvention

a virtual immensity of NOW:ME.
Our big-boned, weanling century drags its heel
between the puddles. Its spillway opens

and closes the rivers
like a kid playing with a lightswitch.
Its cinematic evening hues, its radio shadow

set me humming *The Red River Valley* to the rhythm
of blue snow squeaking beneath my moccasins
in Charleswood. In the dark between houses

where my paper-route's path was a neighbour's trap-line
a rabbit squeals in its wire noose. Beginnings
of the winter constellations rise
and snag in the treetops

ice-up down the tributaries. Canal Flats
sounds more like Missippippi blues
than that land-locked valley ships came through —
first *Gwendoline*, then, in 1902, *North Star*

whose captain blew out the locks' gates
to do it. He blew out the stops
where Thompson portaged

(and would have to portage today
in the silted channel)

while Renoir's purplish horizontals
keep right on doing their gondola impressions
for new money. What are continents, places

when somebody's beachcombing tale is a bottle
of New York mineral water
washed ashore in the Charlottes?

And all of us here via neither
land nor sea, but by body, mystery. . .

My daughter navigating through
a living room strewn with the flotsam
of tinsel and ribbon (an art-class paper angel
in one hand, blue glass star in the other)

slips against me just under my arm holding up
a string of lights I'm testing.
Something's jostled and they come on.

Our awkward hug's brief charm lights up
in the picture window like reflection
in held water. Comes deeply, grandly, true.

Catch And Release

"You're not supposed to watch a tree fall. You have
to turn your back to allow the spirit to escape. Trees
have spirits. Everything has a spirit."

– Mary Hayes, Clayoquot Band

A calm attends October's drowsy creek
suspended in the alder canopy
over the pooled, residual water.

In the bird noise, the sporadic rattling
down of a brittle leaf, you can stand long enough
for crayfish to emerge and proceed, experiencing

every inch of the streambed beneath —
their progress so deliberate and complete

to seem always destination. A shift
of weight to the other foot and there

we are too, self-aware not a second too long
for a view just wide of the minnow. What is it

causes that imperceptible
break in rhythm on the stair, the precautionary
countermanded half-step/almost-stumble

in my mental gait?
Here is thinking gone under bewareness

that nonetheless confesses to intrusion
of its shadow, and a stick's probe

near the reflex. Speedy in retreat
those antennae for trout-rise, the protruding

snout of the turtle, dimple of rain,
exorcise the dry spell, swing back

to the snagged fir in the roped-off area, anticipate
the night of wind and downpour it will crash

through our sleep, the morning of plash
and hustle beneath the bridge we wake

with relief in the next world, the only one
alive to itself and our longing.

Silent, Upon A Height Near Lytton

Long since the north creeks surrendered their gold
and every western island in the stream
is spread-shot glossy in some realtor's dream
we traverse this margin of dry plateau
and Coast Range by highway, not wagon-road
less shadowed in the canyon's sheer extreme.
But opening to grasslands in the clean
wide light, our eyes' long inclination holds
to skyline of that precipice, surmise
that was the soul's high-board, pavilion.
Still thrall to sea-change vistas and wild skies:
its stair, our stare — our techno-odeon.
What's there yawed off-screen on the nighthawks' cries
homing, over the river's undertone?

Through Windfall Centre

in memory of Kristina Kishkan

"The broken mountains have become neutral."

— Carolyn Forché

Its infamous indifference (our difference
that we care and mourn)
can almost hear the boy in me

in the ravine between school and subdivision.
The seminal religion of the weedless lawn
and burr-like bits of botany (fronds

not needles on the cedar, the hemlock's drooping
tip) dipped there into shared irrelevance: waste
ground too steep for building, logged over.
Its second growth was insulation, mossy sponge

for my singular adolescent portion
of anxious longing, coming
to self-consciousness, batting for the personal noises
disallowed everywhere else. And a bafflement

of voice and hearing, place and person
Wordsworthian mutter
                              drones ever on

reinvents its fashion
recycles through orcas or the singing forest
retro-prayer, a sappy public pantheism.
I think to wear with a difference

this Body Shop t-shirt on Father's Day
so you can read it on me if I turn
my back, try to walk away: "Nature

never did betray the heart that loved her . . ."

       ~

Meantime each thing as hard to say
as its form or atmosphere implores of me
metaphor's amber, nocturne, ambivalent specificity.

       ~

Where she died
I've never been but imagine

coastal high country
clear-cut slopes laced
with logging roads and mist.

Granite sky, loose gravel
on the hard turn at lake edge . . .

everything the pre-dawn grey
of the May morning her father phoned
waking us, having waited all night

for a decent hour, unable
to wait longer. She died

and a world in her eyes, behind her eyes
we'll never know, eighteen, planning
to study forestry. I imagine

nothing growing where she died.
The paralyzed moment. No sunrise.

≈

"To cheat," I explain to my curious daughter
and blunder on, "nature won't cheat if you love her,"

enlivening the cruel conceit
it's *our* cheating hearts must belie it to live,
must somehow gladly grasp, bundle

wasp sting, asthmatic
gasp of pollen, bramble dragged
between toes in sandals
                        into the haphazard exhilaration
the pup runs around us, into a sky-diving

caterpillar hope
in its plastic pail
leaf-nurtured, cocooning . . . All

close hurt, hurt aspiration, all
stricture unto death tricks open
tracery, delineation . . .

And opens a roving, rolling eye for distance,
death's princess, demure distraction, a good view

of mountain across the lake, star-shape, spectrum, long
avenue of trees . . .

Her diadem on a foreground bough,
a spring shower's trinket, dangles
the toggle switch

reach/refusal — simplistic riddle
of the light's contrivance.

But thing-bulk and biomass
back of every surface, every assumption
in fleshy O'Keeffe, Carr's turbulence
or Turner's luminosity imply

a problem not for the eye but of the soul.

        ≈

When lilac first by the sundeck rusts
opening summer's reliquary

cottager confronting lake
bends to crank the Merc 150

humbled before the shadowy hills at e'en
and sunset's burnish on the alders

by a wet plug. Of elemental power
pictorial fiction
                 what show him

downwind of the party cutting loose
swathes and swatches of *Purple Haze*
and *Helpless?* Fit requiem

for attention, attachment.
Requiem for scenes imposed
upon the eyes' closing
of things looked at day-long, idly

or in some mild anxiety
of expectation: fragile visibility

of new grass newly watered,
heat sheen of highway

at horizon, thunderheads holding
off. Is that *Stairway*

                 To Heaven clouding
        an Ansel Adams moon
and precipice

warped to the edge, extent
of meaning? Earth, that marble
from Apollo 8, end of the genre?

❧

Soul, the first rung artifice
of consciousness, unseen constant
memory holds sense to seem

clones the lustrous teen
and ornamental cherry blooming
outside the high school, DNA's plausible angels
simultaneous, adjacent

oblivious as I'm driving by
to the codes and processes
shared, their not-so-secret virginities.

How many hidden on the hard drive now
or danced on pinheads then
till we wholly ken that distance, space
itself folds
             into smaller nowhere
             the mind's clothing?

And those ancient forests of physical forms
more medieval daily (present and spectre
and prophecy) take to this new strategy
like logs to water, default

to directory tree, the booms' down-time embroidery
of the river's mouth, pulpy intertexts . . .

    though love for texture likes the leaf
    of another between thumb and forefinger
    wants its transparent apples weighty

and the faller still needs his saw.

Her uncle comes to the funeral
his forehead, hands and forearms bandaged
battered from beating against the windshield

to get back in
underwater
and unknot her seatbelt.

(that apple-cheeked girl)

Whatever she saw disappeared forever
a liquid light.

I'm uncle too, and landholder, believer
after a fashion.

Mother earth, spaceship earth
the firmer than me and you dimension

nothing
where the off-road vehicle goes off land.

≋

Daylight at least. Daylight.
And fireweed flaring in the bleached
and blackened slash, deadfall.

Maybe some buckbrush willow
by the water, clumps

of gangly alder in the gullies
like kids hanging out at the mall.

And the ghost of a moon.

     ❦

Just let me climb up out of this...
spinning my wheels, relentless
pivot of the cycloramic

crowning green neutrality endlessly
shuffling its wild spaces, vistas
into prospects, new perspectives

new age where the worthiest
lie on their backs in the old growth, squinting,
counting murrelets. Omnivores cleaning off

the rose leaves, cleaning up
dropped fruit, even the wasps
have their uses. Mine

incomprehensible, inappropriate here
as right angles, language.
Oh let me climb up out of this

flood of myself, lunacy
of reflection, grotesque in the armoured
circuitry of the virtual

reality harness, vision's bulimic.

෴

Dear wife, lover, love's exclamation
doesn't make us one, but does

bury my face in the burnt-toast smell
of your hair, *my whole heart*

or some such felt
phrase sprung to mind.

So we whisper to each other
aghast now at its toddler charm
your best remembered phrase of hers
coming home in winter, huddled
in all the coats and sleeping bags
as the house thawed: "It's seizing cold
Aunt Terry, seizing cold . . . "

So I've wrestled erect a wall I've framed, spiking
down the braces, or propped the burgeoning

Conference pear, crouched under
its full-term, fruitful shade
overhearing my own seduction.

Skills! Husbandries! Incantations! The struggling
blind entanglements of sorrow, effort, passion!
Everything rests upon them

and their out-sprung gestures, presumptions
of connectedness, unity
played out into . . .
as far as the eye can . . . And this must be

the life of the spirit, echos
of physicality, feeling
cooling its heels

a bodily resonance boding . . .
and foreboding

formal transactions
of material plus gesture: blanket

ceremony, somebody moving
through the windfall centre
as through debris, disaster

to enfold another's shoulders
in the gift, borne . . .

      ℘

awaiting word, wording, received
in the sobs and shudders
                       of the spine collapsing
                  its extension ladder
of amphibian toeholds into gravity

in the self-hug's moan and rocking
in lamentation's shocking self-respect
in the exhaustion of supplication

in body mantra (the monitor's beep
and hum) mind's generator hatching
at last on its flat horizon

a 'happy-face' sticker
or the first Himalayas
of new-sought habitation.
His wavery row

in the gardening therapy plot.

ॐ

Localities, lucidities.

Don't say endangered, dying.
They are done. And stand as they can
in staring, wordless independence

in disproportionate import, icons
of the texts and galleries, decor
of the lobbies and lounges, that portion

of porch steps and railing visible
through a kitchen window

within and outside our fashioning.
We are barely begun, becoming
every ending chased
after "I remember..."

each brush-stroke and f-stop and crippling ellipsis
along the way. Chastened, I laze in flesh tones

in close-ups of the body taken
for Saharan dunes at dawn
or drifts of lunar snow

blunt tongue in the dark
earthy taste of you, the mineral juices —
its life's work bumping into what

might warm to me: the close earth
auditioning, rehearsing us (walk

through to full dress)
for the closing closeness
its choking gasp or sigh

where family throw flowers on the water.

❦

A world to see: not you, not me,
not other, neither
kind nor unkind

emerges from that incidental calm
time (or is it only our time)
finds, belittles, isolates

in glimpses, immeasurable . . .
You wake
                . . . upon a shore
your cheek a little sore from
its position as you dozed

in late summer, late afternoon
on a towel on a log extending
into the lake. A diver

has stepped over you to reach the end.
Everything is close now:
various, explicit, lovely

and committed to itself
and to the contingencies.
Each thing is wise with contingency

and won't say its simple, singular shape,
its colour. Love, work, language

are our business, but
before we are about it, before
we breathe a word or wish

we'd brought the camera, a world
is new, and worth it. Wants us.
It is the world where everything has happened.

Alone In The Water

A kick or two out
against the playful waves

then roll over, look back.
So often I've done this, summers

without number, friends or family
on the shore, a ledge

of rock at Ruby Lake
or Lighthouse Park, trees behind

and above them leaning out
for the open light

and reflected light
and my delight not simply

to be swimming, afloat
but in the perspective

of people in a landscape
beautifully proportioned

enclosed a moment
as though in another room

but present, whole, unencumbered —
the sky always blue

(beach weather) the shoreline reaching
around, away, each way

a point, or cliff, or thicket
of willow, gently emphatic

of the people, their intimate
isolation, approachable

passing a towel or plum
getting comfortable, distant

but undiminished, and I
alone in the water, ambiguously

proud of them, pleased
to swim in and be counted

among them.

Mud Bottom

All day the sea escaping
(the long-legged inlet slipping off her lace)
I catch sight of shining
through the trees and hazy heat

restless as a man awake
beside his sleeping lover.
He lifts the sheet in the moth-soft
whirr and waft of the fan, in curtained light

and gazes at the woman he knows best of anyone
longing to know her. I should put on old runners

to walk the creek's last clarity, its main channel
down the estuary utterly exposed,
brazen and pungent in the sun. Its bed
of clay and hard sand is the only footing
in acres of slippery, deep mud. Its few round stones

in shroud and sweep of seaweed hair are the blind heads
of seekers pushing upstream.
They would be worth knowing, knowing

what a husband knows.
A river, a marriage, living
are deep-pulling puzzlements their whole length.

Where the methodical eagles
took each merganser chick,
where the heron stood
in its private patience

music floats from a weathered float-house above high tide
new wings spread on swell of outcrop and midden.
Added decks (broad leaves unfolded seaward)
kneel, rooted in the water. Its windows bloom

the pale yolk-yellow
of evening primrose in evening shadow.
Where in Pleyel's *Duo* is the hinge

between the crumbled centuries and the violins'
lush harmonies, palatial balconies

where Deva dances? She is three
or five by her held-up fingers
and interrupts my questions

to tell her mother
"I'm just talking to this guy . . . "
A kayak, a passionate pink, skims over
right up to the bottom step to listen.

Exuberant singing from the scarred throat
of a young man no longer
a cancer patient, leads the recent graduates in

>   "I got troubles, whoao oh
>   I got worries, whoao oh
>   I got wounds to bind . . . "

Defiant languor amidst the high sedges
under June's waste of greenery, squeezed
in glossy droplets from the tips
of every seed cone on every fir on the mountain . . .

The stickiness earth is for us
at every turn . . . Quickly sideways

in awkward singularity
crabs in the shallows grab
at prawnshell scraped off our plates.

>   Each makes a little detonation
>   of muddiness in its instinct.

>   "We've done all we can for you,"
>   they say at the clinic . . .

And something mindful, endlessly confronted,
fed and native here ten thousand years (the depth
of fire-blackened, broken shell at wave edge) looks up

(once looked up the names of the early astronomers
who came to the science through music)
and looks down wearing their mantle, leaning
over the railing, evening light on its shoulders

sets aside its scraping tool on the eye-level ledge
to drift in its nebulous, drowning, sacred places
its tombs and temples upstream of Aswan or Three Gorges

drifts against the weave of weir and whale-song
in fire-gazing silences, sounds sources

of relentless presence, gorgeous knowing glances, guesses
at timing, balance

and at a heavier, murky beauty
under each human carapace . . .

teases from selfhood's blackest hole and floodlit reservoirs
a cramped and crabby nebula expanding

luminous excesses, watery losses
of ancient, reflected starlight.

House Posts

One world, here and beyond us
so that reaching for it, into it

hog-ties the shaman blind in his blanket
face-down on the floor, seals out every sliver
of light from the windows to sound the rattles

from everywhere, the muffled voices, sparks
and crescendos erratic in the air. Whether spirits

or apparatus who can say with the fine threads
of the four directions stretched among the supplicants
miraculously intact next morning, and by morning

we're boating, skeptical, talking metaphor, joking.
There's *our* parallel universe: the bluffs

of arbutus and shore pine slipping past,
the island we're approaching friends call

"going to Greece" when we go there
for its shimmering slopes in high summer
of dry moss and gold, flattened grasses,
its hollows here and there as welcoming

as a wife's body, as sharply aromatic.
Wet rock, yarrow, manzanita.

I've no vows, no chanting but this
to hold these shocking constancies, expanses, open

spaces between the trees complete
and sadder than made places . . .

the trees   just where

house posts   would be.

Stepping amidst them, within, I'm over-
hearing my own voice disown me, "yes,

you belong here
but cannot stay."

Watermark

"Here lies one whose name was writ in water"

– Keats

Unimpressed in focus is a deeper sign
not blank to the blind hand on the page
nor propped in light's way shining only

as shone through, relative shadow
to arms-length, optic mind . . .

sister to disappearance. The lake
wind-buffed silver against its current, slips
east in every currency of any time
spent simply knowing . . .

                          undertows the airborne line
                of her arm and upper body stretched
out to the dock to hold us off. Reach, edges

of my life aligned when I stood by the sink unfolding
and folding her letter. Light touch of a quick

word, last word, on the island's spine (silhouette
in breezy, see-through sundress)
nibbles the surface

grazes the girlish
swaying grasses, womanly arbutus, rocky outcrop . . .

veers and flashes going
down dark under pressure, mute
pleasure. Something fishy

persists in the scribble of midges
on monumental air.

Titanic

It was watching Titanic I decided
to give up poetry. It was the moment

when the lovers are struggling
in the flooded compartment or corridor
or in the stairwell having just
escaped the water for the moment
or when they are freezing at sea.

It was one of those moments you know
in a story it's your story, your love, your death
they're living, barely making it

just for the moment clinging
to the rail and the futility

and sadness washed through me, the humiliation.
I was ashamed to have given so much (everything
I could) everything of enormity or not
in my life, to have given it over

to words. Words!
When this was possible:
Big Screen Big Sound, free-

falling off the stern of the century. All around me
thirteen-year-old girls sobbing, Roses afloat
for DiCaprio, so certain

they'd never let go
were letting go. So I gave up poetry

to the shrieking steel and deep ever-ending
ice-burdened kisses. The flat quiet after
under stars. It was one of those moments.

It passed.

Sea Level

"The nature of waters is always to communicate with one
another and to reach a common level. And this is their
mystery."

— Carlos Fuentes

Zero the haughty abstraction blue
sky takes from ocean, blue
ocean takes from sky. Zero my want

of transparency:
world shown to me
shadowed through me.

Zero the hollow eye
of spawned-out coho.

Zero full circle in star-turn and electron
of every middling, conceptual line. Mind at its meal.
A Peace River full of river captured within the sandbags' breached

dominion. Zero theory
and the world this full, blue burgeoning

bull-kelp strand on wave belly . . .
and history a flood

of the lives still coming, each
to fill someone to bursting.
Tenacious, tangential, thirsty as willow

I am rooted at her feet
for the liquor of sweat on her thighs and torso,
for the splendour and drench of arousal,
the body-blow of breaking water.
Lifted, collapsing on the swell

we'll crest on creeks reclaiming Main Street
duck under the arms of the orchards exhausted
with holding up blossom and scent and rain

as under the fires of generations
into the banked and hidden fire
the charcoal streak in the midden

we lap and lick.
Zero, bobbing

duckling on the potent murk, upends itself,
reappears facing elsewhere, rebounding
from root and nutrient (eelgrass,
anemone, fattening fry) a trace of bubbles

where it went under, streaming trace of droplets
where it flaps and skims and rises
from the swirl as in touch as in love.

Acknowledgements

Poems from *Water Stair* have appeared in the following
anthologies, chap-books and periodicals:

Anthology Of Magazine Verse And Yearbook Of American Poetry,
Monitor Book Company (US); *Blossom: An Accompaniment*,
Cobblestone Press; *Canadian Literature*; *Capilano Review*; *Event*;
Fiddlehead; *Fresh Tracks: Writing The Western Landscape*, Polestar
Book Publishers; *Grain*; *The Malahat Review*; *Mud Bottom*, High
Ground Press; *The New Orphic Review*; *Poetry Canada Review*;
Poetry Ireland Review; *Prairie Journal Of Canadian Literature*;
Prism International; *Roothog*, Repository Press; *Rugosa*, Reference
West; *Terrain: A Journal Of The Built & Natural Environments*
(www.terrain.org); *Wetting Our Lines Together, An Antholgy of
North American Fishing Poems*, Tamarack Editions (US); *Witness
To Wilderness*, Arsenal Pulp Press. "House Posts" accompanies
a photograph of the author by Blaise Enright-Peterson and
Barry Peterson in their photo-exhibition of BC Writers, *Lit
Happens!*

Beyond sources identified in epigraphs to the poems I'm
indebted to Simon Schama's *Landscape And Memory*, especially
for his insights into Francesco Colonna's strange and seminal
Hypnerotomachia Poliphili (1499). The philosophic/erotic furore
of Poliphilo's Wet Dream, its deluge of Renaissance energies,
Schama finds channelled and formalized in the river roads and
water stairs of 16th century Italian landscape architecture,
those allegorically saturated progresses from fountain to grotto
to vista, "navigated with the help of mythological and poetic
references." The frontispiece image of *Water Stair* is a wood-
cut, *Poliphilo hears the music . . .* , from Colonna's book.

For their assistance (temporal and financial) in the writing of
these poems, I'm grateful to Capilano College and BC
Cultural Services.